LINER NOTES FOR GETTING OUT WITHOUT CATCHING FIRE

Michèle Saint-Michel

10 9 8 7 6 5 4 3 2 1

Published by Bad Saturn. BAD SATURN and associated logos are trademarks and or registered trademarks.

Ocean cover image by Matt Hardy. Interior photos by the author.

LIBRARY OF CONGRESS
CATALOGING-IN-PUBLICATION DATA
Saint-Michel, Michèle.
Liner Notes for Getting Out Without Catching Fire / by Michèle Saint-Michel.
_ Ist ed.
P
Cr
ISBN: 979-8-9866429-7-0

A clarion call to action, "Liner Notes for Getting Out Without Catching Fire" urges readers to actively engage with the stories of survivors. Michele Saint-Michel picks up the shattered pieces to create a mosaic of experiences and memories in brilliant technicolor. Amidst the collection's electric urgency and quantum slipping, these poems illuminate the indomitable spirit of survivors and the transformative power of feminine relationships, art, and music. Brave, devastating, and essential. Also available in Deluxe (illustrated) edition.

Acknowledgements

"The Immortal Charlie Parker (1955)" as an audio poem in *Lucy Writer's Platform: Disembodied Voices* selection. University of Cambridge, January 2021. Cambridge, England.

Several poems appear as audio works in the experimental documentaries of the *PTSD Suite.* World premiere, October 2020. Berlin, Germany.

"Dead Sea . MAP" in *Flashbacks* film.

"Listen, the Snow is Falling" in *Changes in Mood* film.

"Blocking Beliefs Questionnaire" in *Startle Response* film.

"Metamodernist Still Life" in *Avoidance* film.

"The Death of Cleopatra" in *Trouble Sleeping* film.

"Return of the Unchartable Soul" as poem and film stills in *The Menteur* Literary Magazine. The Paris School of Art and Culture, University of Kent, July 2019. Paris, France.

"There is no parting with sorrow. You'll find tomorrow brings you to return." –Karen Dalton

Now or Never by Billie Holiday and the Count Basie Orchestra (1949)

Not on stage but bathed in purple light
          he's kicking at the bathroom door
the bottom-outside corner
          i cant swallow
my fingers entwine and i lose linear time

i pray to the God of Bathroom Locks
          to the God of Taking Men
          to the God of Sequences and Entanglements

Eternity with fermata
          no answer

But blessed be the Angels of Forgetting
          threadbare thistledown wings
          dull trumpets blare dulcet notes
          in melted praline

          Forget with all your heart
In a jazz club in Kansas City
          the corner outside
18th and Vine
          walls draped in velvet
          air stained thick violet
                    prelude to a happening

The dance floor floods with fine-
    swaying bodies
The players' horns flash and rock
    twist in
    violent choreography
    back and forth

On stage she wails
    the keyhole blinks

Metamodernist Still Life

It's Goya
wide-eyed Saturn eating his sons
a pounce of cats and a magpie on a string

I'm bouncing
between impermanent things

The Dutch get on with it
Moroccans take their time
like ancient Egyptians
and ritualized mummification

ripping strips
of sheets

Rolling me in Spanish red
Flesh spiced with cumin ginger
cayenne and coriander

Drape me over the edge
pincher claw, crusher claw

boiled alive first
embalmed after
the artist feast

Spotless with Transubstantiation

I don't remember dancing in the kitchen
I remember boiling thin noodles alone
I remember the gray microfiber towel I'd worn
a hole in from scrubbing all the surfaces
Every top counter or otherwise excluding
the hood of the gas stove Its grimy layers
became sticky over time Thick with decay

Dirt trapped in amber. I thought
about using the electric drill and affixing
a car detailing attachment and buffing
the thing to within an inch of its life
Exfoliating each bend of steel like toweling
oneself off the week after a bad sunburn

But I didn't. I left it. I'd look at it
each day when I passed Sometimes
I wouldn't register the egg-yolk yellow
coat of grit instead I let my eyes slip
over it. I don't remember dancing
in the kitchen. I remember wringing out
the rust-tinted spaghetti sauce into the sink

Remember watching the scalding mound
of angel hair raised high above his head
the special pasta bowl with blackened-blue
painted tulips And I remember the sound
like a head-on collision as it crashed into tile
tomato sauce and pottery clinging to every
surface

I remember there was no place to hide.

May Day

It's the First of May
outside the Warwick
on Mainstreet. Let's be
lovers he pleads
into the loudspeaker

•

Over time separate words
conjoin. It's howlanguage
operates, and human beings
Makes itself efficient

•

Hiswork isclose to
overflow, comes
close to spillover
andmakes me want
towatch .Likeall
impending .disasters

Today's theday to start anew
path .Firststones looklonely
directionless.need threepoints
tomake aline ...
He asks again, *what*
can I getyou?

•

Trajectory .acceleration
miles betweenme
andtheinseparable .things

When theycome,,it's notalone.it'stogether.
TheTaking men bringdestruction.
Unabletogetoutunabletoplead
speakoutcryoutcryoutcryout
May Day.MayDay! MAYDAY!

Thorn and Steeple and Hives

Not my theory
but theory is I had one
too many

Truth is I wanted to see
to see what would happen
if I let it
                    Let it happen

                    Let all
berries huckle in their
raspiness

                    Let it in again
Azure-black sugary
flame all over
again   Let it
roll down my leg

Let the hive
shutter and vibrate
skin break like dawn
swell
and fester Wash your
feet Wash your feet
Wash your

teeth with your
index finger. Scratch
the truth in the

toothpaste
and spit out all

the seeds

An Occurrence of Multi Temporality

easily lift the sheet like a breeze
leave the lights on

leaves   *stays*

freefall in harness

sold pottery. i never told anyone

it all comes down to belief. Monarch

a lever long enough
a branching:
a. leaf
b. leaf
c. them
d. part
Mistakes can be lethal

even with the lights on. a fluttering

I wasn't 0 1 2 real. Kingdom come

"Pray then this way ..." Matthew 6:9

1. Any reminder Our Father, who
brought back feelings 0 1 2 2. I had trouble
staying 0 1 2 art in heaven, asleep
3. Other things kept making me think
0 1 2 hallowed be your name. 4. I felt
irritable and angry 0 1 2 5. I avoided letting
myself get upset when 0 1 2 I thought
about it or was reminded of My body,
7. I felt as if it hadn't happened or
I wasn't 0 1 2 real. Kingdom come,
8. I stayed away 0 1 2 thy will be done,
from 9. Pictures about it popped
on earth reminders into my mind. 0 1 2
as 10. I was jumpy and easily startled. 0
1 2 12. I was aware that it is in heaven.
I still had a lot of feelings about it,
but I didn't deal with 0 1 2 them.
and 13. My feelings Give us this day
0 1 2 numb. 14. I found myself acting
feeling like I 0 1 2 was back at that time

our daily bread, and 15. I had trouble
falling asleep. forgive us, 0 1 2 16. I had waves
strong feelings about it My body is 0 1 2 our
debts I 17. as we also have tried to remove it
from my memory. 0 1 18. I had trouble
concentrating. 0 1 2 forgiven our debtors. 19.
Reminders of it caused me to have physical
reactions, such as sweating, trouble breathing
0 1 2 nausea, or a pounding And lead us not
into temptation, heart. but deliver us from evil
20. I had dreams 0 1 2 for the kingdom 21.
I felt watchful and on-guard. the power, 0
1 2 22. I tried not to talk about it. and the
glory is yours 0 1 2 forever and ever. Amen

Higgs Field and the Immediate Gravitational Collapse of the Universe

this is a field
reveals soundless vellum skin
                of a long-dead
field-dressed hare
stretched taut

hooked in wire
around adjacent ribs
                cored corpus
strikes torsoless grace

•

this is a leveret
on a Sunday we walk
in the pollen-stuft underbrush
                i'm thinking
where do i start
i'm going to draw a family
tree and cross out all the dead
people she says

a mallet wrapped in blond wool
the pounding begins
            I slip to the end
tenebrous passageway
crossed out and left
to an experience of nature

•

this is a heartland
brittle snail shells held to ears
            never sound of the sea
black-gold topsoil
hide the musky odor of pinks

this is a color field
bury unrooted things
            see what breaks earth
come spring

In the Room of the Draught Miraculous

I

The mother said, I'm so happy
The priest shifted, smiled wider
Diamonds where her uterus should be

II

The doctor said, I'm so sorry
The mother stiffened, held the girl closer
Diamonds where her uterus should be

III

Two by two, they'll come,
sweet nectar to a bee
She'll tire of the mining, the discomfort,
the glimmer
The man said, I'm so sorry
Diamonds where her uterus should be

[Rothko Paints to Mozart in a Room Filled with Atoms] II

No one asks
            how i got in

they all ask the essential
            question: *why*
did I do it?

A better question:
            how am i in two
two places at once?

Floodplain

I love these, I say
Why? Because they are rotted?

No. Because they remind me of childhood
i say and smile at her

Oval with both long sides planed flat
the railroad ties came later, I say

Balance beams of failed olympic dreams
that line the edges of my mother's garden

Dancers don't go to the olympics
nor acrobats nor log cabin river rats

Little girls with brothers who spin rifles
or play league ball

Nor black-gold mud pie bakers
sweatin in the hot surefire of a Missouri sun in July

No medals given out for getting out after high school
not getting pregnant too soon

Working so he can go to technical school
vacuuming up the dog hair

Keeping the grass mowed this year
sitting behind his new love in your old church pew

You've been training your whole life
for this?

To hold your father's waterlogged hand
to watch it happen

To hold it in your belly for a year
in your chest in your lungs and marrow

Keeping the levees from breaking
by not speaking not invoking the devil

To hold it together without failing
hold it up to the light and say

What a pretty kaleidoscope
all the broken pieces make

Scratch climb cling and crawl
marigolds black cherry blossoms

In your hair water moccasins
ungilded river lilies in your mouth

Sweets for a sweetgum
apple blossom from the south

Stretch your mud-caked knees
your rolling swayback to swollen skies

Grow thunderhead confluence haystack
rise a God a giant among three fertile mountains

River bluff pedestals of windswept silos
stuft with feed corn and grain

Rise flood the plain
heart rush to bursting alluvial veins

Look your mother in the face and smile broad
clutch the bouquet

Box elder sycamore river birch and pawpaw
Hawthorn wrapped in rue

Reach into the heavens
open a palm
  like a mouth
  like a bible
  like the lid to the lightning bugs in a bottle
  like hard rain anointing ditch water
Wake

True
Come true

Part 1 2 3

Ball N' Chain by Big Mama Thornton (1968)

he put his heel through
and i

was violent too he'd fall
asleep

id do my best to leave
the room without creating

conjuring a solitary squeak
I left him again

building
                    .blocks.

needle through fabric-
backing-again then fabric again

stitched from uncountable jabs
thimble after thimble-full

quilt blocks muffle
footfalls

Déjeuner sur l'Herbe

A mouth full of daffodils
 ,dandelions ,clover
surprise lilies ,daisies pushing
bushel's full of sun-kissed
noses
 ,bouquets of freckled shoulders
 ,collarbones tied up
in the long shadows made from eyelashes

A hair stuck to my tongue
fish for it with a hooked finger
ear wax coats its tip
pointed blades ,tack chives ,a spade
asparagus
how long has it been
.   odd
how the wrongness pulls me in

Head in my lap ,hands in long locks
pinching earlobes between thumb
          forefinger
fish heads ,vegetable stock ,pearl onions
and breeze Deer sheds ,a trowel ,a brush
past the earth ,plant stems beside
nightcrawlers
 ,worm food cheek by jowl fish bait
brush fresh dirt from the face

Blocking Beliefs Questionnaire

1
For the waltz
we forget the pain in our ankle
and the vision of them leaving
I smell malt beer want to gulp it
when i grow tall and fine
Attract attention. Covered in honey
The sweet stuff I can't get it off

2
It tastes of courage in the
desert and bottles full of ships
and letters and no water to wash it down
thicker than I wish it was
Feet pound out the time
Remove the slippers See the massacre
Hear the music start again

3
Makeshift tap shoes rub
a hole in the tights
two bottles empty while he's gone
swallow 2 3 swallow 2 3 swallow 2 3
The most pleasing art in time
A severed hand on the table
But this isn't art

Three Sheets to the Wind

[They] That's the thing these *they*
[It's hard to talk about [It] drips
[[Sticky] swaying palms honeysuckle
inside inner thighs] Walk under
heaven [*They*?] It's hard to talk
about it [[I can't keep myself]
[safe] inside] Fleshy [skies reflect
I can't keep myself safe]
[[[it's a trick] a trap] [[It's fleshy]
skies reflect [deeper] [beasts]
With no teeth] only it's a
trick a trap Its [tongue [the
moment] [I froze]] [allowed] deeper
Beasts with no teeth Only [let
them Take and [take] shape]
Tongue [the moment] I froze
[allowed [unspeakable acts]][the
laying of hands] [Let them [Take]]
and take [Shape] how to live after
dying] from the unspeakable acts
[the laying of hands] [Walk into the
ocean] [live after dying from the outside in]

Outline [trim the line] Walk into the deep
blue sea [Bathe in your body]
Soft silky fill [Outside in outline]
[Trim [the line] sheets gulp wind]
[Regret it] Your body soft silky
Fill the knowledge in your cup
Sheets [[gulp wind] regret] [[I can't]
hold it] [[Watch it spill] over] the
[knowledge [In your cup] an amber
sacrament] [It can't hold]
[Watch it spill over and over again]
Beasts of burden are [*They*.]
[That's the thing] [these Gods wash the feet
from [sin] drips sticky swaying
Three sheets to the wind]

Manual for Field Dressing

The key to safe and efficient field dressing
is a sharp sturdy instrument

Catch them off-guard or catch their hand
as they walk past catch them unawares

A neg-hit is used to penetrate
a woman's bitch shield

The experienced judge a rack
with terms such as mass tine length
and symmetry rather than strictly
number of points

There are three main groups
her choices (her choice of dress
hairstyle makeup)

her physical characteristics
(how she moves speaks eats)

Expose the breastbone
careful not to injure internal organs

Reach into the cavity and pull
the windpipe loose and her actions
(how she treats others her manners)

A neg-hit can safely be used
to take down a 9 or 10 who knows
she ranks that high

The ultimate shock-and-awe
Anchor the prey with authority

But as always be ready to run
out and finish the job by hand

Catching them is the hardest part

Vigil for the Placebo

It's possible
in
what changed
born again
0 1 2 3 white pills

Just this morning
trees do exist
rising silent as
button roses
decaying
watching 1-3
animals

Then
A muted tessellation
quantum mechanics
2 bathing in artificial
orange blossom

A life raft?
I remember
3 of us plus 1 boundless
What if I break
1 after breakfast 2
dinner 3 before

that's all
my .head.
it's all
viaticum
in foil

I find
on the shore
my body
shone brighter
sheepishly
sunbathing
near the open water

I remember them,,
only
between us
oxygen
in persimmon

I don't remember.
i couldnt fathom
unknowing
the silence
before
the current sweeps us to sea

The Death of Cleopatra

I

he comes in
speaks loan words in French

Foreign tongues
impart dry skin and insides
          what more to say

They bathe her in the foundry

          must cast this Perseus
          from a single mold

When craft becomes art
Ars Ingenio

They throw in pewter
          dishes plates and blades

pulled under the weight of them

A viper couldn't save her
molten the bronze
the Gorgon The artist and the artisan

I.I

and what was there to resist?

Temptation
The Composition of Risk

Not romance. No.
Not romance. Silence

Her stone tongue wags
    tastes the invitation to sense
    erases the topography of resistance
    disturbs all memories of cheek-to-cheek

As cloudless spinal fluid drains
    away all movement
the distance pulls *sors* and siren's call

II

She speaks genius remorseless
  from an asp's lips

  after the first kiss
there is no other

no daughter of deuteronomy

  after charging fills all cavities
They brush away surface impurities

it takes ages
for the new shape
to cool

II.I

For new life adhere to me
    keep nothing

For new life adhere to me
    keep inside voices
    keep the doors locked at all times

For new life adhere to me
    keep it all in--*ad caelum*
    keep the bronze from caking
            the wax from melting
    keep quiet hope for violets
                            for fire poppies
            dust seed over snow

III

Ready the reedless body
    as the altar---a hair's breadth
    for a second life to hold fast

            a carrion crow
            a stork, an oriole

This mother mold is my shelter
My investment. Sprue to the Gods
Carve me over again from burnt umber
            from stone
            from this kiln I am reborn

In this Renaissance
    chase the metal and bury me deep
    blast me with loess sand
    cut away divine threads
            reeds for breath
    weld virgin esse after death

III.I

I am sentinel at sacral center
            where the children still hold their bellies
            and pantomime laughter

I am moored
    leave a coin in shallow water

I am screaming patina
    bow your heads and pray

Listen, the Snow is Falling

noun: giving up; resignation   *verb: give up; resign*

abandonment   abandon
abdication   buckle under
acquiescence   capitulate
capitulation   cave in
cessation   cede
dedition   commit
delivery concede
giving way   cosign
relenting   cry
uncle
relinquishment deliver up
renunciation   eat crow
submission   eat humble pie
white flag   entrust
yielding forego

play dead

Judith and Her Maidservant

Fish fill this river and lies
The fish die in time
Only I stand in the river alive
I've waded out, hiking up my skirts
Barefoot I stand on the altar
Mud between toes, fingerless gloves
She stands on the soggy bank
Holds my bloody sandals

Men fill this river and lies
The men die when I choose
The ripples serpent past
as double-headed eels
The laying on of hands
The avarice in how they want us
The hunger in the wanting
We are all embarrassed to look.

Purity fills this river and lies
The heads of men shift inside
A plaited basket's surface, faces
Gone slack. How else to take
Our power back? I'm shimmering
Judith and what's the true width
And depth of this fishless river
Swimming in glittering death

Current fills this river and lies
The current wild from not sleeping
Ichthys covered in scales of justice
And the Augustine price
Of flooded light---
        a cleansed corpse
        a consolatio for the living
        a baptism for the dead

Back Alley Surgery by Malvina Reynolds (1978)

Secret and thoughtless and unknowing why
we angle our august bodies to the petunia hedge
begin deadheading sanguine blossoms
between forefingers and emphatic thumbs

In the act of making room for what's to come
we pinch away the dead trumpet heads
cleanse celestial bodies in perpetual motion
Pull away damage and the dust of neighboring suns

The forecast burns our retinas as caretakers
chrysalis to the undertaker of swiftly dying planets
and childhood dreams of drying bed sheets on the line

As circumference of creation wraps our waists
the deviation slips its banks upriver
Urgent heliotropic seeds from maple trees
germinate from rooftop gutters

We hold hands and circle the other dial-like
bird-shaped scissors to paradise
hoping the good word gleaned from grapevines
hits the nail on the head

These yarn-eyed Gods hang the sky
with wire coat hangers stretched into diamonds
They measure vast lengths of growing season
They trim edges to stack perfect joyless bundles

We are not moved by our longing
to embody the great nothing
not by the taste of bitter water

After the first frost the petunia hedge rests
atop dry evergreens and dead bushes
living for a while longer before it stops

We drop hands in the autumnal color of silence
quantum time sweeps the unknown peninsula
In the distance the river runs
We part. A wood-nymph takes flight

[Rothko Paints to Mozart in a Room Filled with Atoms] III

Silence* is so accurate
(*A quiet way to say suffocation)

*Part 1 2 **3***

It's So Hard to Tell Who's Going to Love You the Best by Karen Dalton (1969)

I don't think of sex anymore; it's too

I think of the moment the doe emerges
from the wood's edge

Exposing herself to the calamitous
world of men

She is timid but she does not retrace
her steps. I take her in.   Hold her
Quiet. Consuming.   Whole

I don't think of the hunters
        waiting in blinds
        waiting for her to pass
                        to be distracted
I don't give mind to the depth of their wanting

I watch her exquisite form spring to near flight
Watch her devour vast stretches of landscape

Pullulate

I

when we came together
it's face to face and I reach up
to his and he doesn't speak
but he smiles at the end of each
lip like a road that changes
to gravel to a footpath that
leads to the reservoir where
there's all the good fishing

II

it's happened before
carp fishing with my uncle
he mashes together
tight balls of corn flakes
and peanut butter
they like this more
than worms he says
so do I my fingers cling
to one another I pray
each catfish slips its hook

III

before, at Corby Pond
a fishing derby with my
brothers and dad I catch
the first one my bobber
dances on the waves
a tap dance disappears
and breaks my gaze I fight
it's the first time. they
tell me the rainbow creature
the one that sparks
and draws attention away
from my brothers is a sunfish
I ask them how they know
that's how sunfish look he says
throw it back it's a baby

Night Terrors (Reprise) by Diet Cig (2020)

Dimpled glass is opaque
translucent transparent
clear with peach spots
evening looks nearer than sky
the daffodils don't matter

What matters is feeling
cold against hanging curves
mind cleaves to the night
terrors of pears in light
syrup of letting leaving it
open window shade pull
tidal shifting allowing them
close secure the double latch

KnocK KnocK
at the door
Orange you going
to get it?

Moon window in apricot light
swings with small words
peep hole listens for spring
listens as tight sounds uncoil
lyrical syllables fall to earth
treacle bells chime subtle mouth
looks open and closes

KnocK KnocK
at the door
Orange you going to see
who's there?

Brief Trauma History Intake

<Question>
Who do you think you are?
</Question>
<Response>
Daughter of a farmer's daughter reaped
from loess mud Daughter of earth
Daughter of a railroad man's son
</Response>
<ACTION>Bury it</ACTION>

<Question>
What a prize and what's the going price?
</Question>
<Response>
NULL
</Response>
<ACTION>Grow smaller</ACTION>

<Question>
Will you take off the corset?
</Question>
<Response>
Lined not of whale bone
but the cheekbones of my unborn
daughters? Fine, yielding
</Response>
<ACTION>Keep your shit together</ACTION>

<Question>
How much smaller? Can you go smaller?
<Response>
Smaller and smaller
</Response> Smaller. Still smaller.
Smaller. Smaller yet again. Yes, smaller.
Again smaller. No, smaller still. Smaller.
There. Don't </Question>
<ACTION>Don't breathe</ACTION>

<Question>
Where will those legs take you? How
long are they? How often are they kept
crossed? How far can they open?
How fast can they run?
</Question>
<ACTION>*Run!*

<Question>
How will you keep going? Keep
from growing? What happens when it's done?
</Question>
<ACTION>Smile. Show em where you're from

Wake for a Severed Hand

She says *everything Begins with silence*
Reaches into gaping mouths Lifts our wagging tongues
Clips the cords loose from their Foundations watches
how they Curl. fold in on themselves
Origami. Ornaments for the tree.

The Balsam shivers
Snow Floats to rescue us from the Unremarkable cold At
last. Something to talk about. Too shy to clutch the other
To listen to what our Eyes have seen to what our
Shoulders have to say. Carving. Each slice of ham folds
And opens. A crane. A cardinal.

Your young niece says a prayer. Short. Unfeeling. The table
Devoid of lefties, lifts its head Sorrow descends, covers
The bone china in a fine mist. We wipe our cups and sip
Sparkling cider. Fill our mouths Almonds folded in dates
Needles fall to the carpet. Delicate. Yielding.

A trio of angels sings out On high
Porcelain babes don't Fuss, kick, or cry.

Flapping. We rise. Fold our napkins in
Our chairs. A choir. A flock. She slaps down an aged palm
We spread paper wings. Take flight. In pairs

Return of the Unchartable Soul

I

On the day I found out I wasn't whole
I don't recall being upset

Like the time I was told there were planets in the sky
Indeed, that I was standing on a planet in the sky
I trusted the information on blind faith

Each occasion thereafter, when I was
informed of yet further fragmentations
I didn't question the idea
I embodied it as fact

New, factual data
We are part of a galaxy inside a universe.
I've not seen it for myself, yet
I know it to be true.

II

I sip a mercifully strong drink
It's a gimlet with Thai basil
and seawater simple syrup
I stand steps away from heaven
and the Gulf of Thailand

A man makes conversation
with me about his acceptance
into a PhD program in England.
He is to study Philosophy.

I let this wave of information
crash over me:
The irony of a 22-year-old boy
studying Philosophy is not lost on me,
but I remind myself that this man
may be years ahead of his time.

It's impossible to know a person's intentions
at first.

Then, he adds, *it's hilarious, right?*
A PhD in Philosophy?
You do know what
PhD stands for?

III

And I stare into his eager face
and I think of my wedding day
and of editing all of the entrance essays, journal
submissions and resubmissions
the long nights alone
finding condoms in his bag

When I'd go back
when it was *just five more years*
and then we'll be outta here
when he moved out
and spent summers away in Europe
because the stress of the program
was too much

when I took off work
and filled out his applications
and signed his name as mine
and when he finally got his placement
and left to find us an apartment in New York

When I pack our life together
fourteen years of seashells
plucked from beaches
and my grandmother's tea towels
and that chest he bargained for at a yard sale

And I put it all on a truck with great care
and I watch it grow ever smaller
And I don't follow

II

And I hear a wave slap a rock
Quick like the rising tide
I stand before the boy
and I feel the return of my unchartable soul.
The salty water sloshing up the sides of my
cavernous body
capsizing internal organs as the waters rise

Cooling my driftwood-smooth bones
until it whets my drive to stand unwaveringly
to swallow truth that no other man can know
and I look at the boy and without shaking my head
I take a long drink and I lick my lips and say,
No. Tell me.

DOD 5220.22-M

index grabs
            the Sea of Tranquility

the blithe tug introduces sickly sweet
            gravity to the wet oxygen

            of surrender into the clean room
cross my body 3x look both ways lookout

who must be consumed?
            For the physicality of recollecting:

Cronus sandblast the fine epidermis
            write it over 0 1 2 3 4 5 6 7 times

            tacit acquiescence of nothing
the barren truth of forgetting

like clean bones dont sweat honeysuckle
like ill ever get the scent off

Dead Sea . MAP

I'm Not Sure It's Me There, But
Of course
it is.

no reflection nomaps no keys no
direction cardinal no wings
no boat

unknown i float
I've always known
It is

hard for others to go t here. hard to make the leap
They want to make it happen. think it

Couldnt n ever ever happen safer
it is

The not knowing Not the unknown, of course
that's different. It's the not k nowing

A(voi(d)ance). Walking away heave ho Then.
not going in the first time ,place   . couldn't

Study thee water ,cn't recognize mne own . ,compass
Dssctn   . That' s what
.it is rflctn.

Wh's ths ? stalkng splntered frame
bearng a hemsphere .that s

Nghtmres vessel no surprse
,careenng of f course

close both e eyes
you 're t here ,of f course

again .the m again
.it is them, ,again
,of course it is

Born in Flames (1983)

Rocking, a cradle untouched
by a father's baited fingers

in the harp-shaped sea of Galilee
Potential for fast-moving storms

rolling in from Lincoln on wednesday
Pluck out St. Peter's fish, the guppies

and tadpoles. In Rochester Falls
skip feeding the apostles

unhooked obelisk for a nightcrawler
slinking away, shifting sopping ash

The Immortal Charlie Parker (1955)

"Tribe follows tribe, and nation follows
nation, like the waves of the sea. It is
the order of nature, and regret is useless."
–Chief Seattle

She welcomes me in the street
to her home. I arrive early
a trauma response. maybe half
the things i do are. according
to the literature i read. and i read
a lot. there's a lightness that comes
from the understanding of it all–
she's lovely as ever. reminds me
of how her mom was years ago
it is soothing the familiarity of it

we'd had coffee once earlier
donned masks and i took her
to the record store because it's my
sanctuary. stacks in place of pews
sacrement oversized vinyl wafers
the music there is holy this chapel
painted birds flying overhead
plays my favorite hymns. ushers
saints a nun and the rest all sinners

like any hall of worship i suppose
it was the 100th birthday of the Bird
Charlie Parker Kansas City's prince
patron saint of woodshedding
of practice-makes-perfect. i didn't
buy any records as id recently
taken a vow of vinyl abstinence

nothing provokes my anxiety
i like owning things. a trauma response
i read. am told. especially heavy
sacred vinyl sheep. i keep my flock
thin am a bad shepherd a lonely
shepherd she buys a book abt
living into intimacy. we sit in
an empty lot behind an actual church
unmasked distanced physically
socially in all ways   staying
6-feet apart drinking our coffees

she texts her mom
and looks at my teeth a lot
this makes me self conscious
Reminds me of us as children
id asked why her hair was so yellow
admiring it. flaxen hair to me
like winning the lottery
She turned and asked why my teeth
were so yellow. eye for an eye
this cut deep I never said anything
she was younger than me after all

we fall in laughing chums as ever
i tend toward tending her and i try
my best not to do this. we were
child colleagues which is rare
nothing seals your fate
like a dance teacher
with something to prove
and what was that exactly———
what did they need to prove?
and why did they need our bodies
for it? and why did our parents
allow it? and why did we work
so hard? why did we fight tooth
and nail to be accepted as worthy
for sacrifice? we were sheep maybe
or it was some sort of cult. certainly
the closest thing i ever knew to true
religion in fact that's what happened
after i left the religion so did she
and she quickly found a new one:
christianity. that's how we fell out

i told her jesus was santa claus.
i was in college living away
from home for the first time.
everyone I knew killing their deities.
dissolving childhood profits and icons
realizing we'd been fed lies
of who was truly brilliant
extrapolations calculated
from incorrect assumptions.

she'd told me: *I'd rather believe*
what I believe and be wrong,
than believe what you believe
and be right. when i was young
i cared a lot about being right.
far less about being kind.
this feels shameful
was bad coaching was immaturity
a trauma response

go to kmart and buy some guts
our old teacher would say this to us
I was favored for some reason
not all of us were favored
this is how i became the protector
of my yellow-haired colleague
the adults said she was faking asthma
so she wouldnt have to work as hard
i said she wasnt *go back do it again*
no again. no again again no. again.
no from the top! we call it practice
they pick apart every piece of her
i try and fail to keep her safe. why
don't they try to keep us safe?
to protect us from themselves?
why do we have to work so hard
to belong? to be accepted as we are?

she's traded all that in now
for a new religion: progressive socialism
she has many houseplants

a rescue dog and a record player
in the corner she (sadly) doesn't use
i wear my mask in her house
we don't really understand how
this thing spreads yet. i visit after
going to buy the blood coffee
and stopping in at my church
i don't buy any records today either
still on my vow of chastity
we sit in the back, outdoors
they say it is safer. i never feel safe
especially not when i go
to buy coffee having to order
with my back to the door
but it feels safe in her backyard
i feel safe with her

she has tattoos now
and so do i. one of hers
is to honor some brutalist
architecture a sculpture
i dont know if she knows
ive been assaulted or have
ptsd but i begin to suspect
she does when she starts
a conversation that turns
to a discussion of consent.
i was raped by two men
and it feels like it's bold
across my face like a tattoo
a brutalist sculpture

of saint agatha patron saint
of victims of survivors.
from experience people
either want to know
or want to pretend not to

i know ive overstayed
my welcome but it's so nice
to talk about our past careers
as child-ego laborers
we chat about the others
who escaped and the ones
still on the inside
and i know i need to leave
can see the tattoo
showing on her face

when i message her
she doesnt message back
for a few days i think
i mustve said something
offensive or i'm a reminder
of her former faith now abandoned
maybe she didn't mean to have
the conversation about consent.
sometimes people think they can
speak the devil into existence.
a trauma response

she says she might leave the city
maybe I could rent her house
i need a place that's furnished
got rid of all my heaviest things
years back. been unable
unwilling to replace them.
a trauma response. i ask if
she'd like to have a clothing swap
i decided not to buy new clothes
at the beginning of 2020
before the virus started
spreading a new development
in my compulsion toward self-
deprivation a trauma response

i go to her house again. I get
coffee but skip communion this day
we wear masks. drag 8 totes
of clothing up from her basement
she says she's not going to pay
her student loans. as she lifts
i notice her latent muscle tone.
i brought one tote. fretted it was
too much but 8 totes. 8 totes is
something. doesnt sit well in my
guts. 5-6-7-8 totes. jeans are so
heavy. we try things on. it becomes
clear she was being polite
and doesn't want [need]
new [different] clothes

i like to look at how others indulge
themselves. burden themselves?
care for themselves? well, clothe
themselves at least. I take jeans
that are too small (in case i have
a ptsd episode again. stop eating)
a nice coat that fits well. a t-shirt
Ill take the rest to a christian donation
center. give more than i keep
this will feel good like sharing a burden
like erasing a demerit

i cant stop admiring how she is
as an adult. how she is younger
yet *has* so many things so much
debt so much *life* and the benediction
of our in-person exchanges.
with other friends chats are virtual
on zoom or facetime. this is not that.
i doubt it is sacred or special to her
she has a job and yes the boyfriend

she says they sometimes have
an open relationship and i ask why
she would want to do that.
i dont mean to be judgemental
but i wonder why *she* specifically
would want to do that
what the benefits are. i haven't dated
since the person who triggered my ptsd
a wholly ghost, an inconsequential

man, but i think how one can never
really know how people are. a trauma
response and how i wish i could've
seen it sooner a trauma response
and i wonder how i was so blind to it
a trauma response And I tell her i think
things dont happen for a reason but
people come into our lives for a reason
a trauma response I wonder why
i came into her life, I say. she looks away.
i believe I misspoke

I say i'm in the city if she wants to meet.
shes busy. i say i'm visiting an old tree
near her house and she wishes she could
but. i drop some things by her house
i think she might like: some
shoes that remind me of tap shoes
and a sherpa sweater
but she must've missed me.
i say, im looking at studio space
nearby wanna check it out
she agrees but cancels in the end

i text her about once a month
now just to say hello
and ask how she's doing
how her mom is and about her
social justice work

she writes me back a day later
she doesnt ask how i am
maybe its stress, the pandemic
or maybe some people dont come back
into our lives maybe they leave
because they want to.
they grow up survive
the rites of passage
on their own. lose faith in us

this feels heavy. heavy like shame
like a weight of sin of burden
like black-sheep exile
not solitude but loneliness
banishment for cowardice
for leaving for failing to protect them

for christmas i get new socks
two heavy books and a record:
The Immortal Charlie Parker
US release, Savoy Records
i put some things for sale on ebay
as a counterbalance. to lighten
the weight of it make it come out
even. I haven't been to church
in months. decide Ill wait to open
the record. im not sure why

[Rothko Paints to Mozart in a Room Filled with Atoms]

I start dead center
            smack in the middle
of Ochre and Red on Red
            no security at the door
 outside or in
            they cant follow
I slip right in and lose no time

Conjure a lit cigarette and press
            The first goes up so fast

The smell of melting canvas
            triggers a memory
            a savory something
            about foreign coins

            I stand dead center
in all my glory
            on a wooden bench in the Rothko room
at the Phillips
            red as far as the eye can see
            titian walls touch off like kindling
            thick smoke stains my hair

The rest go quicker than i'd guessed
            More akin to a roar than a wail
And, yes, because you asked
            with a certain vehemence*
            like they want me
            to watch them all go
(*A difficult way to say yearning)

Before I know it
            they are all gone

Liner Notes for
Getting Out Without Catching Fire
is a poetry collection by Michèle Saint-Michel
about
leaving / not leaving.

The manuscript was completed at the 92Y Unterberg Poetry Center in New York.

Many of the poems in this collection have titles that share the names of other works of art—including sculptures, paintings, albums, and songs—as well as the names of documents, prayers, processes, places, and named mechanisms of quantum physics. These are utilized in the tradition of ekphrastic poetry.

Some poems evoke other poets through adjacent reference, such as Dickinson's *mantle clock* or Chopin's *musky odor of pinks*, among others.

This is the Standard edition.

The Deluxe edition takes a page from jazz musicians and the bootleg distribution of *The Real Book* of jazz standards.

The Deluxe edition was typeset and then photocopied at the **public library** before receiving its final aesthetic treatment.

This visual treatment limited its distribution and resulted in the creation of this more legible Standard edition.

The Standard edition is also available as an eBook.

The book serves as the liner notes for
the experimental music album
Getting Out Without Catching Fire.

Please support the following musicians
responsible for sonically responding
to the poems in this collection:

Sophie Stone

Sheena Dham

Hermon Mehari

Lina Dannov

Arun Sood

Sylvia Hinz

Eryk Salvaggio

James Fella

Silvia Cignoli

Listen to the album anywhere you stream music.

Michèle Saint-Michel
is an artist, filmmaker, and author.

Her experimental films and art books bend genre. Designed to promote healing, her works encourage healthy coping after difficult experiences.

After the heartfelt reception of *Grief is an Origami Swa*n, Saint-Michel released the experimental poetry collection, *Saint Agatha Mother Redeemer* and accompanying coloring book.

She's also released a set of journals based on the writing of Walt Whitman.

Her installation films have been exhibited in galleries and art festivals worldwide.

When she isn't creating art books and films, she's tending her land art piece [poetry forest], and pressing flowers.

Michèle Saint-Michel was born in Kansas City, Missouri. Before moving to London, she worked from a log cabin nestled among the rolling hills and river bluffs of the Missouri River in America's heartland. For now, Saint-Michel works steps from the River Thames.

Also from Michèle Saint-Michel

Grief is an Origami Swan:
An Art Book About Grief

Saint Agatha Mother Redeemer:
A Survivor's Story in the Words of Dead Poets

Saint Agatha Mother Redeemer
Coloring Book

A Journal of Gigantic Beauty

Experiments in Dreaming

Journeywork of the Stars

Liner Notes for Getting Out Without Catching Fire:
Deluxe Edition

Available anywhere you buy books, but we encourage supporting local, indie booksellers.

www.ingramcontent.com/pod-product-compliance
Lightning Source LLC
Chambersburg PA
CBHW030509130626
46549CB00007B/2910